PRAYERSCRIPTS
Speaking God's Word Back To Him

THE PRAYER OF JABEZ

MAY YOUR HAND BE WITH ME

30 Days of Prayers For

LIVING UNDER DIVINE POWER AND

PRESENCE

CYRIL OPOKU

May Your Hand Be With Me: Living Under Divine Power and Presence

© 2025 Cyril Opoku. *PrayerScripts*. All rights reserved.

Published by *Quest Publications*

ISBN: 978-1-988439-83-9

Cover design by *Quest Publications (questpublications@outlook.com)*

Unless otherwise indicated, all Scripture quotations are taken from the World English Bible WEB, which is in the public domain. For more information, visit: www.worldenglish.bible

This book is a work of devotional encouragement. It is not intended to replace biblical study, pastoral counsel, or professional therapy.

Printed in the United States of America.

First Edition: August 2025

For more books like this, visit *PrayerScripts:* https://prayerscripts.org

CONTENTS

Contents..*iii*

Preface .... *v*

How to Use This Book...*vii*

Introduction ....*x*

Week 1: The Guiding Hand of God.. 1

Day 1:   Enlarge My Steps...2

Day 2:   Let Your Hand Help Me 4

Day 3:   Fear Not, I Am With You 6

Day 4:   The Good Hand Upon Me 8

Day 5:   Destiny Secured by His Hand..10

Day 6:   Counsel and Instruction 12

Day 7:   Held by His Hand...14

Week 2: The Strengthening Hand of God..16

Day 8:   Supernatural Strength Released......................................17

Day 9:   The Sound of Strength...19

Day 10: Lifted by His Spirit 21

Day 11: Hearts Strengthened Together.......................................23

Day 12: Everlasting Arms Uphold Me 25

Day 13: Strength for the Weary 27

Day 14: Clinging to His Hand...29

Week 3: The Empowering Hand of God 31

Day 15: The Hand of the Lord With Me 32

Day 16: The Lord Was With Joseph 34

Day 17: The Lord Was With Samuel...36

Day 18: Anointed by the Spirit 38

Day 19: The Lord Was With David..40

Day 20: Anointed With Power...42

Day 21: Your Right Hand Glorious 44

Day 22:   The Right Hand of Victory 46

Week 4: The Preserving Hand of God.. 48

Day 23:   Marked by God's Hand.. 49

Day 24:   Upheld by God's Hand.. 51

Day 25:   Engraved in God's Hands 53

Day 26:   Secure in God's Grip 55

Day 27:   Preserved by Divine Favor.. 57

Day 28:   Protected by God's Hand.. 59

Day 29:   Life in God's Hand... 60

Day 30:   Fear Not, He Holds Me 61

Epilogue 63

Encourage Others with Your Story.. 65

More from PrayerScripts... 66

PREFACE

"For the hand of the Lord my God was on me, and I
gathered men out of Israel, chief men, to go up with me."
— Ezra 7:28 WEB

The hand of the Lord—it is the difference between failure
and favor, between defeat and destiny fulfilled. In my own
walk with God, I have seen that when His hand is upon a
person, doors open that no man can shut. Strength rises where
weakness once prevailed. Guidance comes in the midst of
confusion, and protection surrounds even in the fiercest battles. His
hand is not just a symbol of power; it is the very expression of His
presence resting upon His children.

As I began to write this book, *May Your Hand Be With Me*, my heart
burned with the same cry that Jabez lifted before God. Like him, I
long to live under the covering of God's hand—walking in His
strength, moving by His guidance, and resting in His protection.
This book was birthed not just from study, but from a deep desire
to experience and help others experience what it means to live
under divine power and presence daily.

You will find in these pages prophetic prayers anchored in
Scripture. They are not written merely as words to read but as
spiritual weapons to wield. Each prayer is a cry for God's hand to
lead you into victory, to guard your family, to enlarge your territory,
and to secure your destiny against every adversary. My prayer is
that as you engage these words with faith, you will sense the mighty

hand of God lifting, sustaining, and establishing you in every area of life.

May this book become your companion in seasons of weakness, your strength in battles unseen, and your guide as you press into the fullness of God's plan. Above all, may the testimony of your life be this: *The hand of the Lord was with me.*

Under His Mighty Hand,
Cyril O. *(Illinois, August 2025)*

HOW TO USE THIS BOOK

This book is designed as a daily companion to guide you into a prophetic lifestyle of prayer. This is not just a devotional; it is a prayer journey meant to position you to walk in the fullness of God's promises. Here's how to make the most of it:

1. Dedicate a Daily Time:

Set aside a consistent time each day to engage with the prayer for that day. Treat this as sacred time with God, where distractions are minimized, and your heart is fully focused on communion with Him. Ten to twenty minutes daily is sufficient to meditate on the Scripture, pray, and receive revelation.

2. Begin with Scripture Reflection:

Each day begins with a carefully selected Scripture. Read it slowly, meditate on its meaning, and let the Holy Spirit illuminate how it applies to your life. Allow the Word to penetrate your spirit and prepare you to pray from a place of faith and expectancy.

3. Pray the Guided Prayer:

Use the prayer provided as a framework, allowing it to resonate with your own words and personal circumstances. Speak each declaration with authority and confidence, fully believing that God is enlarging your borders, breaking limitations, and establishing your territory. You may also pause to personalize the prayer for your specific family, career, or ministry needs.

- **Make It Personal**

  These prayers are written in the first person so you can make them your own. Speak them aloud, inserting the names of your family members, your workplace, your church, or your city where applicable. The more you personalize the prayer, the more you will sense its power shaping your reality.

- **Pray with Authority**

  These are not timid requests; they are bold decrees. Lift your voice as a covenant child of God, covered by the blood of Jesus and backed by heaven's authority. When you pray, do so with confidence that Christ has already won the victory on your behalf.

- **Leave Room for the Holy Spirit**

  These written prayers are a guide, not a limit. As you pray, pause to listen. The Holy Spirit may give you prophetic words, insights, or specific instructions. Follow His lead. Allow Him to expand the prayer, add declarations, or guide you into deeper intercession.

4. Journal Your Insights:

Keep a notebook or journal to record any thoughts, revelations, or confirmations you receive during prayer. Writing down what God speaks to you helps solidify understanding and creates a record of breakthrough and growth over time.

5. Repeat as Needed:

Some prayers or themes may need to be revisited multiple times. Answer to prayer is progressive; the more you engage with these prayers in faith, the greater the manifestation in your life and household. You can return to this book at any season to reinforce your victory and dominion.

6. Live in Expectancy:

Prayer is only one part of walking in enlargement—your actions, faith, and obedience amplify the power of these prayers. Move boldly into opportunities, embrace the doors God opens, and live with a confident expectation that God is answering your prayer beyond what you can see or imagine.

By following this guide daily, you will cultivate a lifestyle of prayer and kingdom impact. Let this book be your companion as you step into the new dimensions God has destined for you.

INTRODUCTION

"Jabez called on the God of Israel, saying, 'Oh that you would bless me indeed, and enlarge my border! Let your hand be with me, and keep me from evil, that I may not cause pain!' God granted him that which he requested."
—1 Chronicles 4:10 WEB

When Jabez lifted his prayer to heaven, he uttered a cry that still resounds across generations: *"Oh that You would bless me indeed, and enlarge my border! Let Your hand be with me..."* (1 Chronicles 4:10). He understood something most people miss—the blessing of God is incomplete without the hand of God resting upon it. Enlargement without His hand leads to collapse; success without His hand leads to sorrow. But when the hand of God is with a person, every blessing is preserved, every boundary is secure, and every step is guided into destiny.

The hand of the Lord represents His tangible presence in the life of His people. Throughout Scripture, the mighty hand of God is seen delivering Israel from bondage, guiding His prophets, empowering His servants, and preserving His chosen ones. It is His hand that stretched out the heavens, divided the Red Sea, strengthened Elijah to outrun Ahab's chariot, and anointed the apostles to heal the sick and turn cities to Christ. That same hand is still at work today—guiding, strengthening, empowering, and preserving all who call upon His name.

In my journey with God, I have discovered that nothing compares to living under the weight of His hand. His hand steadies you when the ground beneath you feels shaky. His hand lifts you when trials threaten to crush you. His hand directs you when paths seem uncertain, and His hand covers you when the enemy rises like a flood. To live under God's hand is to live under divine power and presence, walking in a security that no human effort can provide.

This book, *May Your Hand Be With Me*, is an invitation to walk under that hand daily. It is more than a collection of prayers; it is a spiritual roadmap into a life covered, empowered, and sustained by God Himself. The prayers here are designed to be prophetic weapons—crafted from the Word of God, sharpened by the Spirit, and aimed at destroying every enemy of your destiny. Each week carries a theme that reflects a unique dimension of God's hand in your life.

In **Week One: The Guiding Hand of God**, you will discover how His hand directs your steps, establishes your path, and leads you into the place of promise. When you feel lost or uncertain, His hand becomes your compass, ensuring you will not miss your way.

In **Week Two: The Strengthening Hand of God**, you will be equipped to receive courage in the face of fear, resilience in times of trial, and supernatural strength in seasons of weakness. His hand is the source of renewed power when your own resources have run dry.

In **Week Three: The Empowering Hand of God**, you will encounter the anointing and equipping that comes from His presence. His hand is what transforms ordinary men and women into vessels of extraordinary impact. When His hand empowers you, no enemy can resist, and no obstacle can prevail.

In **Week Four: The Preserving Hand of God,** you will experience the security of being carried, covered, and protected. His hand shields you from destruction, sustains you through storms, and ensures that what He has begun in you will be completed.

This is not just another devotional. It is a call to live under open heaven, to invite the same hand that shaped the universe to shape your life. It is an opportunity to partner with God in prayer and position yourself for the undeniable evidence of His hand upon your family, your work, your ministry, and your destiny.

As you journey through these prayers, approach them with faith and holy expectation. The hand of the Lord is mighty to save, strong to deliver, and faithful to uphold. May your life carry this eternal testimony: *"The hand of the Lord was with me, and nothing could stop what He had purposed for my life."*

Now, let us step together into the place of divine power and presence. May His hand be with you.

WEEK 1:
THE GUIDING HAND OF GOD

Theme: God's hand directs, leads, and establishes your steps.

There is no greater comfort than knowing the hand of the Lord is guiding your every step. Life is filled with decisions, crossroads, and moments of uncertainty. Without divine direction, it is easy to wander in circles or waste years pursuing paths that lead to frustration. But when God's hand is upon you, He leads you into the right doors, connects you to the right people, and establishes your steps in righteousness. His guidance is not vague; it is precise, purposeful, and filled with wisdom that cannot fail.

The guiding hand of God is what kept Israel through the wilderness with a cloud by day and fire by night. It is what led Joseph from the pit to the palace, and it is what has directed countless men and women of faith into their destinies. His hand not only shows you where to go but also keeps you from paths of destruction. When God is your compass, you will never be lost.

As you journey through this first week, expect to see the Lord take hold of your path in a fresh way. These prayers will help you surrender fully to His direction, silence every confusing voice, and invite the Spirit of God to counsel you daily. The hand that carved out the heavens is the same hand ready to hold yours and lead you safely into the place He has prepared.

DAY 1

ENLARGE MY STEPS

Jabez called on the God of Israel, saying, "Oh that you would bless me indeed, and enlarge my border! Let your hand be with me, and keep me from evil, that I may not cause pain!" God granted him that which he requested.
— 1 Chronicles 4:10 WEB

O God of Israel, the One who answers by fire and shows mercy to those who cry out, I lift my voice to You with holy boldness. Let Your mighty hand rest upon me and my household. Stretch forth Your arm to bless me indeed and to enlarge the borders of my life, so that no adversary can contain or restrict the destiny You have ordained for me. I refuse to live in smallness, limitation, or bondage, for Your hand sets me free to walk in divine enlargement.

By Your power, I trample upon every enemy that seeks to cage my life. Break the cords of evil conspiracies designed to narrow my influence, diminish my light, or silence my voice. O Lord, lift the boundaries of my dwelling and cause me to inherit the land You have appointed. Let the grip of wickedness shatter under the weight of Your presence.

I declare that my steps are ordered by the hand of the Almighty. Every demonic blockade standing at the threshold of my enlargement is crushed. Witchcraft embargoes and generational curses collapse before the consuming fire of Your Spirit. My family shall no longer be hindered by cycles of failure or stagnation.

Father, keep me from evil. Let no weapon fashioned against me prosper. Guard my name, my health, my children, and my legacy under the covering of Your hand. I will not bring pain; I will not be trapped in sorrow. Instead, I rise to be a channel of blessing in the earth.

You are the God who enlarges my steps so that I will not slip. Let every field of influence You entrust to me be fruitful. From today, let nations be touched by the overflow of my life. Let my borders testify of Your power, and let Your name alone be glorified.

In Jesus' name, Amen.

DAY 2

LET YOUR HAND HELP ME

Let your hand be ready to help me, for I have chosen your precepts.
— Psalms 119:173 WEB

O Father of Lights, whose hand never fails, I call upon You to release the fullness of Your help into my life. I have chosen Your Word, I have embraced Your precepts, and I will not turn aside to the paths of darkness. Now, O Lord, stretch forth Your hand to lift me above every adversary. By Your mighty right hand, deliver me from snares and strengthen me to walk uprightly before You.

I decree that no power of hell shall prevail against me, for Your hand rests upon me for good. Every trap of deception, every net of confusion, and every snare of compromise set against me and my family is scattered by the fire of Your presence. Lord, let Your hand defend my household, shielding us from sudden attacks of the enemy, visible and invisible.

Arise, O Lord, and let every enemy of my soul flee. Where evil hands are stretched against my destiny, let them wither and fail. Where dark powers try to manipulate my pathway, let Your hand redirect my steps into victory. My help is not in human strength but in Your hand that upholds the universe.

Father, surround me with Your divine assistance. Strengthen my spirit to obey, sharpen my mind to discern, and empower my heart to remain steadfast in righteousness. I will not be swallowed by trouble. I will not be overthrown by trials. Instead, I will emerge stronger, upheld by the grip of Your hand.

Let generations know that I stand because of Your help. Let my children inherit the testimony that God's hand fought for us, lifted us, and preserved us. My life shall declare Your unfailing help in every season.

In Jesus' name, Amen.

DAY 3

FEAR NOT, I AM WITH YOU

Don't you be afraid, for I am with you. Don't be dismayed,
for I am your God. I will strengthen you. Yes, I will help
you. Yes, I will uphold you with the right hand of my
righteousness.
— Isaiah 41:10 WEB

Mighty God, my refuge and fortress, I exalt You for Your unfailing promises. You are the One who upholds me with Your righteous right hand. I refuse to bow to fear or intimidation, for Your presence drives away dread and strengthens my heart. With Your hand upon me, I walk boldly into my destiny, unshaken by the threats of darkness.

Father, break every chain of fear woven by the enemy to cripple my faith. I silence every voice of doubt that whispers despair into my spirit. By the authority of Your Word, I declare that terror, anxiety, and confusion shall not prevail in my life or in my family. Instead, the power of Your hand lifts us above oppression into the place of victory.

Let Your righteous hand shield me from the plots of the wicked. Where my strength fails, let Your strength abound. Where my courage wanes, let Your Spirit rise within me. I am not abandoned; I am upheld by the Everlasting One whose hand spans the heavens and crushes the plans of my adversaries.

I proclaim that my household is preserved under the banner of Your hand. Every assignment of destruction, every arrow of fear, and every storm of discouragement is rendered powerless. Your hand steadies me, Your hand fights for me, and Your hand delivers me.

Lord, I arise in confidence, knowing You have already secured the victory. My life shall not be governed by fear but by faith. My steps are fortified, and my heart is established because You are my God and You uphold me always.

In Jesus' name, Amen.

DAY 4

THE GOOD HAND UPON ME

The king granted me, according to the good hand of my
God on me... I told them of the hand of my God which
was good on me, as also of the king's words that he had
spoken to me. They said, "Let's rise up and build." So they
strengthened their hands for the good work.
— Nehemiah 2:8,18 WEB

Sovereign Lord, the Builder of destinies, I thank You that Your good
hand is upon me. When Your hand rests upon a life, favor flows,
doors open, and divine help appears. Just as You granted Nehemiah
success in the presence of kings, let Your good hand empower me
to rise and build everything You have purposed.

I decree that every adversary seeking to frustrate my assignment
shall be overthrown by the weight of Your hand. No spirit of
opposition shall hinder the building of my life, my family, or my
destiny. The evil conspiracies of Sanballat and Tobiah against my
progress shall collapse in shame. Your hand secures victory over
resistance and accelerates the fulfillment of Your promises.

Father, breathe strength into my hands for every good work. Anoint
me to complete what I start. Let divine resources flow, let helpers of
destiny arise, and let every provision be released under the covering
of Your hand. I shall not labor in vain, nor shall my family be cut
off in the midst of building.

O God, establish the work of my hands. Preserve me from discouragement, and silence the voices of opposition. Where men conspire to weaken me, let Your Spirit empower me to rise higher. Your good hand is my guarantee of success, and Your presence ensures my triumph.

My testimony shall be that the hand of the Lord has done it. Let generations know that I rose and built because of the favor of my God. By Your hand, I am established, and by Your hand, my destiny shall be fulfilled.

In Jesus' name, Amen.

DAY 5

DESTINY SECURED BY HIS HAND

All who heard them laid them up in their heart, saying,
"What then will this child be?" The hand of the Lord was
with him.
— Luke 1:66 WEB

Everlasting Father, I glorify You for the power of Your hand that shapes destinies. When Your hand rests upon a man, his life carries prophetic weight, and his destiny shines with divine purpose. Lord, let Your hand be with me and my household, marking us as carriers of destiny that cannot be denied.

I cancel every demonic handwriting of limitation written against my family's future. I silence every evil voice that questions our destiny. O Lord, let the assurance of Your hand silence the doubts of men and the accusations of the enemy. May every child in my lineage bear the evidence of Your covering and walk in the fulfillment of divine purpose.

Lord, I refuse to live as ordinary. Your hand sets me apart, consecrates me, and empowers me. By Your hand, every assignment from heaven concerning me shall come to pass. No enemy shall truncate my purpose, and no force shall derail my journey. I am marked by heaven and sustained by Your hand.

Father, establish my household as a prophetic testimony in the earth. Let every gift You have placed within us blossom under the covering of Your hand. Let nations marvel and ask, "What shall this one be?" For they will see the undeniable evidence of Your presence guiding our path.

By Your hand, secure my destiny. By Your hand, preserve my heritage. By Your hand, release victory in every battle. O God, let my life declare that Your hand was with me from beginning to end.

In Jesus' name, Amen.

DAY 6

COUNSEL AND INSTRUCTION

I will instruct you and teach you in the way which you
shall go. I will counsel you with my eye on you.
— Psalms 32:8 WEB

Faithful Father, I honor You as the One who leads and teaches me
by the power of Your Spirit. Your hand does not leave me to wander
in confusion, but it guides me in the path of righteousness and
victory. Lord, open my ears to hear Your instruction, and guide me
into the way of destiny that You have appointed.

Every voice of deception speaking contrary to Your Word is
silenced now. I shall not be misled by the counsel of the wicked.
Every demonic manipulation designed to derail my path is
overthrown. Lord, with Your eye upon me, I am preserved from
destruction and directed into fruitfulness.

I decree that my family and I shall walk under the counsel of the
Most High. Where others stumble in darkness, Your light shall
shine upon us. Where others grope without direction, Your hand
shall guide us to green pastures and still waters. We are instructed
of the Lord, and we shall not fail.

Father, dismantle the schemes of the enemy that attempt to confuse
my steps. Let every crossroad be illuminated by Your Spirit. Teach
my hands to war, my heart to discern, and my feet to walk securely.
My life shall not be wasted on wrong paths or vain pursuits.

O Lord, be my unfailing Counselor. Govern my decisions, align my steps, and let my life glorify You. By Your hand, I will not miss my season. By Your counsel, I will arrive at the place of promise.

In Jesus' name, Amen.

DAY 7

HELD BY HIS HAND

Nevertheless, I am continually with you. You have held my
right hand.
— Psalms 73:23 WEB

O Eternal God, I exalt You for holding me continually by Your
hand. When others forsake me, Your grip never loosens. When the
storms rage, Your hand steadies me. You have not allowed me to
slip into destruction, for You hold me fast. Lord, let this
unbreakable hold preserve me and my family all our days.

I decree that no power of darkness can snatch me out of Your hand.
Every evil hand stretched forth to seize my destiny is broken by fire.
Every satanic grip upon my household is shattered by the mighty
hand of the Lord. I am untouchable, secured in the palm of the
Almighty.

Father, keep me close, and never let me drift away. Surround me
with Your covering presence, and preserve me from the snares of
the enemy. I renounce every covenant that binds me to defeat, and
I embrace the covenant of Your hand that leads me to victory.

Lord, let my life be a testimony of one held firmly by God. In every
season—whether in joy or trial—Your hand remains faithful. I will
not stumble into the pit of destruction, for You are my Keeper. I
declare that my children, my household, and my heritage are held
by the everlasting hand of God.

From this day forward, let it be said that I am sustained, guided, and preserved by the hand that rules the universe. You are my confidence and my strength forever.

In Jesus' name, Amen.

WEEK 2:
THE STRENGTHENING HAND OF GOD

Theme: God's hand imparts strength, courage, and resilience in weakness

Every believer will face moments when human strength runs out. Life has a way of pressing us beyond our natural capacity—through trials, battles, and challenges that would break us without divine intervention. It is in these moments that the strengthening hand of God becomes our greatest ally. His hand not only carries us when we are weak but infuses us with supernatural strength to keep moving forward.

The same hand that strengthened Elijah to outrun the chariot of Ahab is the hand that empowers you to rise above the weight of adversity. When the enemy comes like a flood, the Spirit of the Lord lifts up a standard against him, and His hand becomes your shield and your strength. Weakness is not the end when God's hand is upon you; it is the very place where His power is made perfect.

This week, you will learn to draw upon the limitless strength of God. These prayers will stir you to cast off fear, rise above discouragement, and receive fresh courage for your journey. The hand of the Lord will not let you collapse in the midst of trial—it will steady you, strengthen you, and carry you to victory.

DAY 8

SUPERNATURAL STRENGTH RELEASED

"Yahweh's hand was on Elijah; and he tucked his cloak into his belt and ran before Ahab to the entrance of Jezreel."
—1 Kings 18:46 WEB

Mighty God, I rise today in the power of Your hand that came upon Elijah. Just as You enabled him to outrun the strength of kings and horses, I declare that Your supernatural energy courses through my body, my spirit, and my destiny. I will not be slowed down by the weights of fear, fatigue, or oppression, for Your hand propels me forward with divine speed.

O Lord of Hosts, I break every spiritual chain that has tied me to delay, stagnation, or exhaustion. Let every enemy pursuing my family be left behind in the dust of defeat. Your hand strengthens my feet like those of a deer, and I will tread upon high places where no adversary can reach. I decree that every wicked plan assigned to weary me shall be overturned by Your hand of power.

Father, You are my strength when I am weak. As You came upon Elijah, come upon me now with prophetic acceleration. Let the fire of Your Spirit consume every obstacle that dares to stand in my path. My household shall not faint; we shall finish strong.

Today I arise under the divine unction of Your Spirit. My spirit is ignited, my strength is renewed, and my destiny is advanced. No enemy can restrain me, for Your hand is mighty upon me.

In Jesus' name, Amen.

DAY 9

THE SOUND OF STRENGTH

"When the minstrel played, Yahweh's hand came on him."
—2 Kings 3:15 WEB

Sovereign God, I call upon You with a song of victory in my heart. As the minstrel played and Your hand fell upon the prophet, I declare that as I worship, Your presence rests mightily upon me and my family. Music stirs Your Spirit, and under that anointing, divine strategies for triumph are released.

Lord, every atmosphere of heaviness around me is shattered by the sound of praise. Every demonic voice of confusion is silenced as Your Spirit hovers over me. I will not walk in the counsel of the wicked, for the sound of heaven guides my steps. Let every plan of darkness be exposed and dismantled by the melodies of Your Spirit.

O God, as David's harp drove away tormenting spirits, so let the atmosphere of worship in my home drive out oppression, depression, and every unclean power. Let Your hand rest on me as I lift my voice in praise, causing my enemies to scatter seven ways.

Father, I decree that my family's environment is saturated with Your presence. Songs of deliverance surround us; prophetic insight flows freely. Under the canopy of Your hand, I will never walk in defeat.

I rejoice, for Your hand strengthens me as I worship. From today, I move forward with divine confidence and clarity, sustained by the music of heaven and the power of Your Spirit. In Jesus' name, Amen.

DAY 10

LIFTED BY HIS SPIRIT

"So the Spirit lifted me up, and took me away; and I went in bitterness, in the heat of my spirit; and Yahweh's hand was strong on me."
—Ezekiel 3:14 WEB

O Mighty Deliverer, I thank You for the strong hand of the Spirit that lifted Ezekiel. When bitterness tried to pull him down, Your hand strengthened him. Today, I decree that Your hand is strong upon me, lifting me from every weight of oppression, sorrow, and despair.

Lord, no bitterness shall root in my heart, no heaviness shall hold me captive, and no demonic burden shall tie down my destiny. Your hand strengthens me in my spirit, empowering me to walk boldly into the assignments You have given me. Every weapon formed against me and my household shall be consumed by the fire of Your Spirit.

Father, I speak prophetically over my life: I will not be bound by the heat of anger, resentment, or grief. I rise above every attempt of the enemy to weaken my faith. Your hand lifts me, sets me on solid ground, and establishes my steps in righteousness.

O God of power, I decree that my family is carried by Your hand into safety. We are preserved, elevated, and carried into divine purpose. No power of darkness shall bring us down, for Your Spirit strengthens us beyond natural ability.

I walk forward under the weight of Your glory, upheld by the strength of Your hand, unstoppable in my assignment, and victorious in battle.

In Jesus' name, Amen.

DAY 11

Hearts Strengthened Together

"Also the hand of God came on Judah to give them one heart, to do the commandment of the king and of the princes by Yahweh's word."
—2 Chronicles 30:12 WEB

Great King, I exalt You for the unifying power of Your hand. As You moved upon Judah to give them one heart to obey, so I declare that Your hand rests upon me and my family, bringing divine unity, harmony, and strength to stand together in Your will.

Father, every spirit of division, confusion, and strife sent against my household is destroyed by the fire of Your Spirit. We shall not be scattered by the enemy's schemes, but bound together in the love of Christ. Your hand strengthens us to walk in one accord, to resist evil, and to pursue holiness.

O Lord, make my heart steadfast in Your Word. Empower my family to align our desires with Yours. Let no adversary exploit weakness, for in unity we stand strong, fortified by Your hand. I decree that every force plotting to scatter, separate, or weaken us is bound and cast down.

God of covenant, Your hand gives us strength not only to resist the enemy, but to advance Your kingdom together. We rise as one in prayer, in purpose, and in obedience. Your hand shields us from attack and equips us with courage to walk in destiny.

By the power of Your hand, I declare my family unbreakable, unshakable, and unstoppable in the purpose of God. We will walk together in divine strength, fulfilling every command You have spoken.

In Jesus' name, Amen.

DAY 12

EVERLASTING ARMS UPHOLD ME

"The eternal God is your dwelling place. Underneath are
the everlasting arms. He thrust out the enemy from before
you, and said, 'Destroy!'"
—Deuteronomy 33:27 WEB

O Eternal God, I bow before You, my dwelling place and fortress.
Your everlasting arms are stretched beneath me, lifting me above
danger and carrying me through every storm. You are my sure
foundation, and no enemy can overthrow me.

Lord, I decree that every adversary standing before me is thrust out
by Your mighty hand. No satanic trap, no generational curse, and
no demonic stronghold shall prevail. Your arms shield me, and in
Your authority, I declare destruction to every plan of wickedness
against my life and my family.

Father, let Your everlasting arms break the grip of fear and
oppression. As You command "Destroy," I rise in holy boldness,
demolishing strongholds, tearing down altars of darkness, and
overturning evil decrees. My household is hidden in the refuge of
Your arms, untouched by calamity, preserved for glory.

God of eternity, You carry me when I am weary, sustain me when I
am faint, and strengthen me for battle. The enemy will not triumph,
for Your arms hold me secure. I decree that every force rising
against my children, my work, and my destiny is scattered by the
thrust of Your mighty hand.

Today, I rest under the canopy of Your everlasting arms, confident, strong, and victorious. No enemy shall prevail, for You, O Lord, are my eternal dwelling.

In Jesus' name, Amen.

DAY 13

STRENGTH FOR THE WEARY

"He gives power to the weak. He increases the strength of him who has no might…those who wait for Yahweh will renew their strength. They will mount up with wings like eagles. They will run, and not be weary. They will walk, and not faint."
—Isaiah 40:29-31 WEB

Almighty God, I lift my hands to You, the Giver of power and strength. You empower the faint and renew the weary. Today, I declare that my strength is renewed by the hand of the Lord. I will soar above adversity, rise above attacks, and walk in victory without fainting.

Lord, every arrow of weakness launched against my body, soul, or spirit is shattered. Every plan of the enemy to weary me or my family is overturned. The fire of Your Spirit infuses me with energy, resilience, and divine courage. I decree that my house shall not collapse under pressure, for Your strength sustains us.

Father, lift me as on eagle's wings, above every storm of confusion, above every flood of affliction, and above every plot of darkness. Let the hand of the Lord shield me from fatigue, empower my steps, and fortify my spirit.

God of might, I decree that my family will not faint. Our prayers will not be silenced, our hands will not grow weak, and our faith will not waver. We shall run the race of destiny, fueled by Your Spirit, and finish strong in Your glory.

By Your mighty hand, I am renewed, uplifted, and unstoppable. Strength flows into me now, and I walk boldly in triumph.

In Jesus' name, Amen.

DAY 14

CLINGING TO HIS HAND

"My soul stays close to you. Your right hand upholds me."
—Psalm 63:8 WEB

O God, my soul clings to You with desperation and devotion. In the midst of battle, I declare that I will not let go of You, for Your right hand upholds me. You are my strength, my security, and my salvation.

Lord, every enemy that seeks to pull me down is defeated by the grip of Your hand. No demonic force, no generational curse, and no wicked decree can snatch me from Your hold. Your hand stabilizes me in weakness, lifts me when I stumble, and carries me when I cannot walk.

Father, I decree that my family is upheld by Your hand. We will not be shaken, we will not be moved, and we will not be destroyed. Your hand shields us from danger, silences the voice of the accuser, and establishes us in righteousness.

O Upholder of my soul, let every storm be stilled as I cling to You. Let every adversary scatter as Your hand strengthens me. My life is not in the grip of the enemy but in the everlasting grasp of my Redeemer.

I declare prophetically: I will cling to You all my days. Your right hand upholds me, preserves me, and leads me into my destiny with power and peace. In Jesus' name, Amen.

WEEK 3:
THE EMPOWERING HAND OF GOD

Theme: God's hand anoints, equips, and empowers for service and victory.

God never calls without equipping, and He never sends without empowering. The hand of the Lord is the seal of divine empowerment upon His servants. It is His hand that anoints, equips, and authorizes you to walk in victory and to fulfill your kingdom assignment. Without His hand, human efforts crumble. With His hand, the impossible becomes possible.

From Moses to the apostles, Scripture reveals that the empowerment of God's hand transforms ordinary lives into vessels of extraordinary influence. The hand of God was upon Gideon, and he defeated the Midianites. The hand of God was upon David, and he brought down Goliath. The hand of God was upon the early church, and entire cities turned to the Lord. When His hand rests upon you, your words carry weight, your prayers carry fire, and your life becomes a testimony of His power.

As you pray through this week, expect a fresh impartation of divine empowerment. These prayers will activate the gifts within you, release boldness upon you, and clothe you with the anointing needed to overcome every adversary. The hand of the Lord will equip you for service and usher you into victories you could never achieve on your own.

DAY 15

THE HAND OF THE LORD WITH ME

The hand of the Lord was with them, and a great number
believed and turned to the Lord.
— Acts 11:21 WEB

O Lord of glory, I stand under the covering of Your mighty hand,
the same hand that moved in Antioch and caused multitudes to
turn to You. Let that same hand rest upon me and my household.
By Your power, every resistance of darkness against our faith and
destiny is crushed.

Father, let Your hand break through every veil of deception around
my family. Cause scales to fall from eyes, and let hardened hearts
melt before Your Spirit. May Your hand arrest every power that
blinds, binds, and resists our obedience to Christ. By Your mighty
touch, release revival fire within us, and let the fragrance of Christ
spread through our lives.

Lord, as Your hand empowered the early believers to triumph,
empower me to advance in righteousness. Let no scheme of the
enemy prevail. Cancel every demonic contract, uproot every
satanic altar, and silence every voice raised against my destiny. May
Your hand raise me above all adversaries.

Let the weight of Your presence rest upon my home, my work, and
my ministry. By Your hand, secure my borders and frustrate the
wicked who plan evil against me. May every spiritual chain fall, and

every gate of bronze shatter. Lord, let many witness Your glory through me and be drawn into Your Kingdom.

I decree that my life will bear witness to the greatness of Your hand. My family shall be signs and wonders, and the enemy shall bow under the power of the risen Christ. In Jesus' name, Amen.

DAY 16

THE LORD WAS WITH JOSEPH

Yahweh was with Joseph, and he was a prosperous man. He was in the house of his master the Egyptian. His master saw that Yahweh was with him, and that Yahweh made all that he did prosper in his hand... But Yahweh was with Joseph, and showed kindness to him, and gave him favor in the sight of the keeper of the prison... the keeper of the prison committed to Joseph's hand all the prisoners who were in the prison. Whatever they did there, he was responsible for it. The keeper of the prison didn't look after anything that was under his hand, because Yahweh was with him; and that which he did, Yahweh made it prosper.
— Genesis 39:2-3,20-21,23 WEB

Faithful Father, I lift my voice in bold declaration: because Your hand is with me, no chain, no pit, and no prison can hold my destiny captive. The same hand that lifted Joseph from slavery to rulership rests upon me and my household.

Lord, in every place where the enemy has sought to limit me, let Your hand bring prosperity and favor. As You made Joseph fruitful in the house of bondage, make me fruitful even in seasons of trial. Let Your hand distinguish me in my workplace, my community, and among nations. May the fragrance of Your presence announce me, and the evidence of Your favor silence every accuser.

Every prison gate the enemy has erected against me is shattered by Your power. Let every false accusation, every evil conspiracy, and every demonic manipulation fall powerless before the authority of Your hand. Cause every crooked place to be made straight, and lift me into the place of divine appointment.

O God of covenant, let my life reflect Your favor. Like Joseph, let everything committed into my hands prosper. Cause my family to walk in excellence, integrity, and divine covering. Let our story proclaim the glory of Your presence with us.

I decree today: I am untouchable under the hand of the Almighty. No enemy plan can halt my rising. My future is secured in the hand that never fails. In Jesus' name, Amen.

DAY 17

THE LORD WAS WITH SAMUEL

Samuel grew, and Yahweh was with him, and let none of
his words fall to the ground.
— 1 Samuel 3:19 WEB

Sovereign Lord, I lift my voice in thanksgiving that Your hand rests
upon me, even as it rested upon Samuel. By Your hand, establish
me as a vessel of truth, power, and authority in this generation.

Let every word I speak be sharpened by Your Spirit. May none of
my declarations fall void, but let them strike down the works of the
enemy and plant the purposes of heaven. Lord, empower my voice
to silence the lies of darkness and to release life over my family, my
community, and my nation.

Father, I reject every scheme of the wicked designed to render my
voice powerless. I destroy every spiritual gag placed upon my
mouth. By the hand of the Almighty, I decree that my utterances
carry the weight of heaven. May my intercessions tear down
strongholds and my decrees establish Your will in the earth.

Just as Samuel's life was a testimony of Your presence, let my life
radiate Your glory. Let Your hand shield me from every snare, and
may my path remain steadfast in holiness. Protect my family from
every devourer, and cause our testimonies to multiply as proof of
Your covenant presence.

I decree that I walk in prophetic accuracy, divine authority, and
unstoppable influence. The word of the Lord in my mouth shall

break chains and release destinies. By Your hand, I shall never be silenced. In Jesus' name, Amen.

DAY 18

ANOINTED BY THE SPIRIT

Then one of the young men answered, and said, "Behold,
I have seen a son of Jesse the Bethlehemite who is skillful
in playing, a mighty man of valor, a man of war, prudent
in speech, and a handsome person; and Yahweh is with
him."
— 1 Samuel 16:18 WEB

Lord God Almighty, I declare that by Your hand, I am set apart as
David was, marked by skill, valor, and wisdom. Your presence upon
me makes me a mighty vessel, anointed for battle and excellence.

Father, let the testimony of my life be that the Lord is with me. May
every enemy who observes my rising know that it is not by might
nor by power but by the Spirit of the Living God. Let the fragrance
of Your presence draw favor into my life and terrorize the powers
of darkness that seek to resist me.

Every spirit of insignificance, obscurity, and limitation, I cast you
down by the authority of Christ's blood. The same hand that lifted
David from the fields of Bethlehem into the palace lifts me from
obscurity into divine visibility. Lord, make me a vessel of wisdom
in speech and courage in warfare.

Let Your hand anoint me for excellence in every assignment. May
my skills shine in the marketplace, my voice carry weight in
leadership, and my courage defeat every Goliath standing against

my destiny. Lord, let Your hand make me a solution-bearer in my generation.

I decree today: my life carries the seal of divine presence. No adversary can overthrow the testimony that the Lord is with me. My destiny is preserved and my victories are guaranteed. In Jesus' name, Amen.

DAY 19

THE LORD WAS WITH DAVID

Saul was afraid of David, because Yahweh was with him,
and had departed from Saul.
— 1 Samuel 18:12 WEB

Mighty God, I proclaim with boldness that because Your hand is with me, every adversary shall fear. As David's presence unsettled Saul, so shall my life trouble the forces of darkness that rise against me.

Father, let Your hand be the shield of my family. Cause every power that seeks to oppress, manipulate, or destroy us to flee in terror. As Your presence departed from Saul, let the presence of every wicked pursuer depart from their schemes. Let confusion be their portion and defeat their inheritance.

Lord, clothe me with the armor of Your Spirit. Let my obedience, like David's, command respect and establish dominion. Where envy and jealousy are stirred, let Your hand establish me so firmly that no plot can dislodge me. Silence every whisper of slander and every tongue of accusation.

Let Your presence with me be a consuming fire against my enemies. May every arrow launched in secret return upon the heads of those who sent it. Cause the fear of the Lord to fall upon every adversary, and let my victories multiply as testimony of Your hand upon my life.

I decree that I walk in untouchable favor. Because the Lord is with me, no enemy can prevail. My household is secured, my future is preserved, and my destiny is unstoppable. In Jesus' name, Amen.

DAY 20

ANOINTED WITH POWER

Even Jesus of Nazareth, how God anointed him with the
Holy Spirit and with power; who went about doing good
and healing all who were oppressed by the devil, for God
was with him.
— Acts 10:38 WEB

O Father of Lights, I rise in the authority of Christ, declaring that
the same Spirit and power that rested upon Jesus now rests upon
me. By Your hand, I am anointed to destroy the works of darkness
and to bring deliverance to the oppressed.

Empower me, O Lord, to carry healing in my hands and deliverance
in my words. Let every trace of oppression in my family be
shattered. Break the chains of sickness, fear, and bondage. Cause
the devil's grip to be loosed, and let liberty flow in abundance.

Lord, may my life reflect the ministry of Jesus—doing good,
healing the broken, and setting captives free. Wherever I step, let
Your hand go with me. May demonic powers tremble and flee at the
sound of Your name in my mouth. Let miracles, signs, and wonders
testify that the Lord is with me.

I break every generational curse, every yoke of delay, and every
satanic cycle. The anointing destroys them now. Lord, let the power
of Your Spirit turn my home into a fortress of peace and my life into
a testimony of victory.

I decree today that I am a carrier of heaven's power. I will heal, restore, and liberate by the hand of the Almighty. My destiny is unstoppable because God is with me. In Jesus' name, Amen.

DAY 21

YOUR RIGHT HAND GLORIOUS

> Your right hand, Yahweh, is glorious in power. Your right
> hand, Yahweh, dashes the enemy in pieces.
> — Exodus 15:6 WEB

Almighty Warrior, I exalt Your mighty hand that shatters the enemy
in pieces. As You fought for Israel against Pharaoh, fight for me
today. Let Your glorious right hand arise against every adversary of
my destiny.

Lord, break in pieces the demonic altars raised against me. Let the
sorceries of darkness collapse under the weight of Your power. May
every oppressor of my family be dashed to fragments before Your
hand. Lord, fight for me, and let the spoils of victory be my
inheritance.

Father, let Your right hand establish my authority in the land of the
living. Place me in a secure place above the reach of the enemy.
Cause every plot of witchcraft, sorcery, and enchantment to
backfire. Let Your right hand be my weapon of defense and offense.

With Your hand upon me, I march into my inheritance. No Red Sea
shall stop me, no Pharaoh shall enslave me, and no army shall
defeat me. Your hand ensures my deliverance and guarantees my
victory.

I decree today that my life is upheld by the right hand of power.
Enemies will fall, and I shall rise triumphant. My family shall walk

free because Your hand dashes the adversary into pieces. In Jesus'
name, Amen.

DAY 22

THE RIGHT HAND OF VICTORY

The voice of rejoicing and salvation is in the tents of the
righteous. "The right hand of Yahweh does valiantly. The
right hand of Yahweh is exalted! The right hand of Yahweh
does valiantly!"
— Psalm 118:15-16 WEB

Lord of Hosts, I lift my voice in triumph, declaring that the right
hand of the Lord does valiantly in my life. Your hand is exalted
above every enemy power, and Your victories resound in my
household.

Let songs of deliverance fill my home, O God. Where the enemy
planned sorrow, let there be rejoicing. Where despair sought to
settle, let salvation spring forth. Cause my tent to resound with
testimonies of Your right hand at work.

Lord, let every adversary of my family be defeated. May the sound
of their downfall echo louder than their threats. Where curses were
spoken, let blessing arise. Where darkness covered, let Your
glorious light break forth. Your hand ensures my victory.

Father, establish a covenant of joy in my lineage. May every battle
fought result in rejoicing. Cause my name to be associated with
triumph and my household with victory. Let all who see me know
that the right hand of the Lord has prevailed.

I decree today: the voice of rejoicing will never leave my home. My tent shall always resound with the sound of salvation, for the right hand of Yahweh does valiantly. In Jesus' name, Amen.

WEEK 4:
THE PRESERVING HAND OF GOD

Theme: God's hand sustains, protects, and carries you into destiny.

The journey of life is filled with battles, but the hand of the Lord is our guarantee of preservation. His hand does not only guide and strengthen—it sustains, protects, and carries us safely into destiny. Without His preserving hand, the enemy would have swallowed us up long ago. But because His hand is upon us, we are shielded, defended, and kept from destruction.

The preserving hand of God is what carried Noah through the flood, Daniel through the lion's den, and the three Hebrew boys through the fiery furnace. It is what kept Paul through shipwrecks and persecutions, and it is what will keep you and your family today. His hand is not short that it cannot save, nor is His power weak that it cannot preserve.

This final week will anchor you in the security of God's covering presence. These prayers will silence every attack against your life, break the grip of premature death, and release the assurance that God Himself is carrying you into destiny. With His hand upon you, no power of darkness can cut short what He has ordained. You will live, you will endure, and you will finish strong—preserved by the mighty hand of the Lord.

DAY 23

MARKED BY GOD'S HAND

"This man came to him by night, and said to him, 'Rabbi, we know that you are a teacher come from God, for no one can do these signs that you do, unless God is with him.'"
— John 3:2 WEB

O Lord of Glory, the One who walks with power and manifests wonders, I declare that Your hand rests upon my life. Just as Your presence distinguished Jesus and testified through undeniable signs, so let Your hand mark me, my household, and all that concerns me. I refuse to live unseen by heaven or uncovered by Your Spirit. Let the evidence of Your hand upon me be undeniable, that every adversary will know You are with me.

Father, I thank You that Your hand is not hidden nor weak. Let it distinguish me in the midst of trials, lifting me from obscurity to a place of testimony. Every spiritual enemy seeking to diminish my light or obscure my destiny, let the fire of Your hand consume their plots. As You empowered Your Son with signs and wonders, empower me to walk in such divine manifestation that the kingdom of darkness trembles at the mention of my name.

By the authority of Jesus Christ, I break off every assignment of shame, reproach, and limitation against me and my family. Let Your hand preserve us from the snares of the wicked. Mark us with favor in every season of life. Father, let every eye see that You are with us, that every tongue is silenced, and that Your power is glorified through us.

Let my life be a living testimony that Your hand is mighty to save, mighty to heal, mighty to protect, and mighty to deliver. Today I walk boldly under that covering, knowing no enemy can prevail against what You have sealed with Your hand.

In Jesus' name, Amen.

DAY 24

UPHELD BY GOD'S HAND

"Even there your hand will lead me, and your right hand
will hold me."
— Psalm 139:10 WEB

Almighty Father, my Keeper and Sustainer, I proclaim that no
matter where life carries me, Your hand is faithful to guide and
uphold me. You are the God who charts my steps and ensures I am
never abandoned to the will of the enemy. Even in dark valleys,
Your right hand grips me with unshakable strength, ensuring that I
cannot be lost.

Lord, let every evil plot against my family be scattered by the
holding power of Your hand. Where the enemy seeks to push us
down into despair, let Your hand lift us up. Where arrows fly against
our health, peace, and destiny, let Your hand cover us as a shield.
Preserve us from the schemes of those who hate righteousness, and
let the power of Your grip crush every force of darkness contending
for our souls.

I decree that no place is beyond Your reach. In my going out and
coming in, in the night hours and in the breaking of dawn, Your
hand sustains me. Every satanic ambush is nullified by the hand
that leads me forward. Lord, do not allow my steps to slip or my
destiny to derail.

Father, I rest in the assurance that Your hand will never release me
to destruction. Hold my children, my spouse, my loved ones firmly

within Your grasp. Lead us through stormy waters into the safety of Your promises. Let our enemies watch as we flourish under Your hand of preservation.

In Jesus' name, Amen.

DAY 25

ENGRAVED IN GOD'S HANDS

"Behold, I have engraved you on the palms of my hands.
Your walls are continually before me."
— Isaiah 49:16 WEB

O Lord, Eternal Keeper, I glorify You because I am inscribed upon Your hands. No power of hell, no decree of man, no curse of the enemy can erase me from Your remembrance. Your eyes are ever upon me, and Your hand is my place of safety.

Today I rise with boldness, declaring that I and my family are untouchable because we are engraved in Your palms. Every force of wickedness that seeks to scatter our walls, let them fall by the power of Your hand. Let every accuser that rises against us be silenced by the mark of Your covenant. We are not forgotten; we are preserved by Your mercy.

Lord, where enemies seek to tear down our protection, rebuild our walls with Your glory. Fortify our lives with divine strength. I decree that the storms of life will not consume us, because our foundation rests in the palm of Your hand. Even if the world forgets us, You, O God, have bound us to Yourself in unbreakable love.

Father, I thank You that my children, my household, and my destiny are written into Your palm. Every evil hand stretched against us with intent to harm will be broken, for Your hand alone secures us. Preserve us with power that cannot be erased.

I live with confidence that my name, my calling, and my future are sealed in the hand of the Almighty. Forever remembered, forever preserved, forever safe.

In Jesus' name, Amen.

DAY 26

SECURE IN GOD'S GRIP

"I give eternal life to them. They will never perish, and no one will snatch them out of my hand. My Father, who has given them to me, is greater than all. No one is able to snatch them out of my Father's hand."
— John 10:28-29 WEB

Father of Eternity, the Shepherd of my soul, I declare that I am safe in Your grip. My family is secure in the palm of Your hand. No demon, no adversary, no witchcraft, no curse can pry us away from Your grasp. We belong to You, preserved by the blood of Jesus Christ.

Lord, I dismantle every demonic attempt to steal, kill, or destroy what You have entrusted to us. No snare of the enemy will prosper. Your hand is our fortress, Your hand is our refuge, Your hand is our covering. I decree that we shall not perish but live and testify of Your preserving power.

O Mighty God, where the enemy comes as a roaring lion seeking prey, let Your hand strike him down. Where unseen forces plot against our health, marriages, children, and future, let the authority of Your hand scatter them. We are untouchable because Your hand preserves us with eternal strength.

Thank You, Lord, for the assurance that You and the Father hold us in a double grip that no power can break. We rest in this unshakable truth: we are sealed, secured, and preserved forever. In Jesus' name, Amen.

DAY 27

PRESERVED BY DIVINE FAVOR

"Now God made Daniel find favor, compassion in the
sight of the prince of the eunuchs."
— Daniel 1:9 WEB

O Lord, who opens doors no man can shut, I declare that Your hand of favor is upon me and my family. Just as Daniel was preserved and lifted by divine compassion, so let Your hand distinguish us in every sphere of life. Where others see resistance, may we see the hand of favor breaking through.

Lord, I call down judgment upon every enemy assigned to block my advancement. Let every wall of opposition crumble before the favor of Your hand. Every voice that speaks against me at the gates of opportunity, let them be silenced by the evidence of Your presence.

Father, I thank You that favor is not dependent on man's decision but flows from Your hand. Surround me with compassion that shields me from destruction. Where envy rises, let Your hand subdue it. Where manipulation seeks to derail my path, let Your hand redirect me into destiny.

I decree that my family walks in undeniable favor—at work, in school, in ministry, in business, and in the land of our dwelling. Let Your hand mark us as chosen, blessed, and preserved. O God, release angelic help that confirms Your favor upon us.

May we flourish where others fail, rise where others fall, and remain unshaken in the face of trial, because Your hand sustains us with unending compassion.

In Jesus' name, Amen.

DAY 28

PROTECTED BY GOD'S HAND

"For I was ashamed to ask of the king a band of soldiers
and horsemen to help us against the enemy in the way,
because we had spoken to the king, saying, 'The hand of
our God is on all those who seek him, for good; but his
power and his wrath is against all those who forsake him.'"
— Ezra 8:22 WEB

O Lord, my Protector and my Shield, I proclaim that Your hand
rests upon me for good. Just as Ezra testified, so do I: the hand of
God covers those who seek Him. I refuse to trust in the arm of flesh,
for Your hand is stronger than any earthly guard.

Father, let every enemy that waits on the journey of my life be
scattered by the force of Your hand. Let every ambush, every trap,
every demonic patrol against my destiny be destroyed. I decree that
Your hand preserves my family from the violence of the wicked.

Lord, when fear whispers of danger, let Your hand silence it. When
adversaries plot in the dark, let Your hand shine light that blinds
them. I stand under the covenant of preservation that says no
weapon formed against me shall prosper. Your hand is my ultimate
defense.

Father, I release my journey, my household, and all that concerns
me into Your hand. May Your goodness surround us as a shield. Let
Your wrath dismantle every opposing force, and let Your favor go
before us. In Jesus' name, Amen.

DAY 29

LIFE IN GOD'S HAND

"Who doesn't know that in all these, the hand of Yahweh has done this, in whose hand is the life of every living thing, and the breath of all mankind?"
— Job 12:9-10 WEB

Sovereign Creator, the One who holds the universe, I declare that my life and the life of my family are in Your hand. Every breath we take is sustained by You, and no force of darkness can steal what You preserve.

Lord, I dismantle every demonic spirit of death, sickness, and destruction sent against us. Because our lives are in Your hand, I decree that we shall not die before our time. No curse of premature death, no attack of sudden disaster will snatch us away. The hand of Yahweh preserves our years.

Father, in Your hand is not only life but destiny. Mold us into the vessels You desire. Guard our health, our wealth, and our future. Let the adversary find no access point into our lives. Where the destroyer lurks, let Your hand shut the door.

I release every worry, every fear, and every uncertainty into the hand that created me. I live with confidence that my family is preserved, my children are secured, and my tomorrow is written in Your palm.

Lord, let our enemies see that our lives are untouchable, for we dwell in the hand of the Almighty. In Jesus' name, Amen.

DAY 30

FEAR NOT, HE HOLDS ME

"When I saw him, I fell at his feet like a dead man. He laid his right hand on me, saying, 'Don't be afraid. I am the first and the last.'"
— Revelation 1:17 WEB

Alpha and Omega, the First and the Last, I bow before You in awe and trembling. Yet, in my weakness, Your right hand rests upon me. Your touch drives away fear, silences torment, and revives my soul.

Lord, where the enemy seeks to paralyze me with fear, let Your hand empower me with courage. Let the terrors of the night and the arrows of the day be scattered by the authority of Your touch. When I feel overwhelmed, remind me that Your hand is steady and unfailing.

Father, I release my family under the covering of Your hand. Let no fear, no confusion, no chaos rule over us. Touch our lives with power that breaks the yoke of fear. Every satanic intimidation assigned against us, let it crumble before the hand that holds the keys of death and Hades.

I decree that I will not live as a captive to fear, but as a warrior sustained by Your presence. Your hand has the final word over my destiny. You are the beginning and the end, the keeper of my days.

Let Your hand rest upon me until every shadow of fear departs and every enemy bows to the name of Jesus. In Jesus' name, Amen.

EPILOGUE

As you have journeyed through these thirty days of prophetic prayers, you have lifted the same cry that Jabez once prayed: *"Oh, that You would bless me indeed and enlarge my territory!"* This is not a cry of ambition, but of alignment—a call to step into the inheritance God already prepared for you before the foundations of the world. By faith, you have broken limitations, shattered barriers, and declared enlargement over your life and family.

Enlargement is not a one-time experience; it is a lifestyle of continual stretching. Every time you pray, believe, and act on God's Word, He pushes back the borders of confinement and opens new doors. Expansion is progressive—what you walked into today is only a foretaste of the greater spaces God is leading you into tomorrow. The enemy may attempt to resist, but remember: once God enlarges your borders, no power of darkness can confine you again.

As you move forward, keep declaring these prayers. Let them become the language of your spirit. Expect fresh territories in your walk with God, in your relationships, in your influence, and in your provision. Live with the conviction that God has called you beyond limits, destined you for fruitfulness, and appointed you to leave a legacy of enlargement that will echo through generations.

Go forth in faith. Step boldly into greater spaces. Walk in fruitfulness and overflow. And may your life forever testify of the God who hears, the God who enlarges, and the God who establishes. Your territory has already been marked by His hand. Now, arise and possess it.

In Jesus' name, Amen.

ENCOURAGE OTHERS WITH YOUR STORY

If this prayer guide has strengthened your faith, deepened your intercession, or helped you stand in the gap, would you consider leaving a short review on Amazon? Your feedback not only encourages others but also helps more believers discover this resource and join in the prayer movement. Every review—just a few sentences—makes a difference. Thank you for being part of this movement.

MORE FROM PRAYERSCRIPTS

COMMAND YOUR DESTINY SERIES

Command Your Morning:

30 Days of Prayers and Declarations to Seize Your Day and Shape Your Destiny

There is a battle over every morning—and every believer must choose to either drift into the day or command it.

Command Your Night:

30 Days of Prayers and Declarations to Secure Your Rest and Shape Your Tomorrow

Every night is a spiritual battlefield—what you do before you sleep can determine the course of your tomorrow.

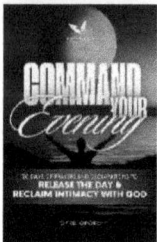

Command Your Evening:

30 Days of Prayers and Declarations to Release the Day and Reclaim Intimacy with God

There is a battle over every transition—and evening is one of the most spiritually neglected.

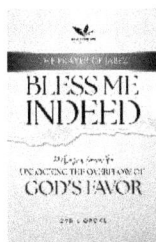

Bless Me Indeed:

Unlocking the Overflow of God's Favor

What if you could activate God's favor in your life today and walk in blessings that surpass your wildest expectations?

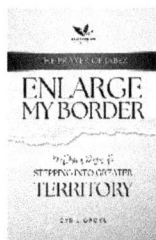

Enlarge My Border:

Stepping Into Greater Territory

Do you feel like you're living beneath your full potential? Do limitations, setbacks, and invisible barriers keep you from stepping into all God has promised? It's time to lift your cry for enlargement.

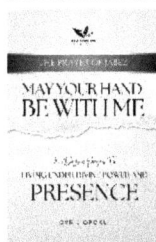

May Your Hand Be With Me:

Living Under Divine Power and Presence

What happens when the mighty hand of God rests upon your life? Doors open that no man can shut. Strength rises where weakness once prevailed. Guidance comes in the midst of confusion, and protection surrounds you in every battle.

Keep Me From Evil:

Standing Untouchable in Spiritual Warfare

What if the enemy's plans could never touch you or your family? Imagine walking through life completely protected, untouchable, and victorious—no matter what schemes are formed against you.

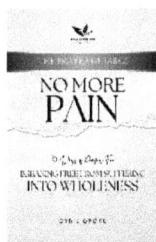

No More Pain:

Breaking Free from Suffering into Wholeness

Have you been carrying the weight of sorrow, disappointment, or hidden wounds for far too long? Do cycles of pain seem to repeat in your life, your marriage, or your family?

	Discern the Enemy:
	Sharpening Spiritual Perception to Recognize Satan's Tactics and Guard Your Destiny
	The greatest danger is not the enemy you can see—it is the one you cannot. Can you recognize the enemy before he strikes?

	Disarm the Enemy:
	Stripping Satan of Weapons and Influence Through the Power of Christ
	Are you tired of feeling like the enemy has the upper hand in your life? It's time to take back your ground, silence the lies of darkness, and walk in the unstoppable authority of Christ.

	Destroy the Enemy:
	Breaking Strongholds and Cancelling Evil Works by God's Authority
	Are you tired of living under the weight of unseen battles? It's time to rise up and destroy the enemy's works in your life.

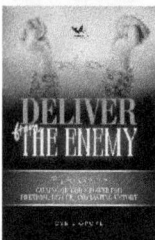

	Deliver from the Enemy:
	Calling on God's Power for Freedom, Rescue, and Lasting Victory
	Break free from spiritual attacks and experience God's mighty deliverance in every battle.

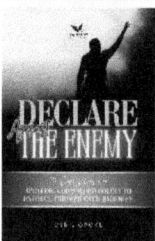

	Declare Against the Enemy:
	Speaking God's Word Boldly to Enforce Triumph Over Darkness
	What if you could silence the enemy's schemes, protect your family, and walk boldly into every God-ordained assignment with unshakable authority?

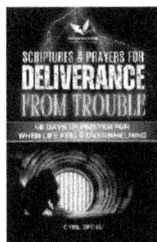

Scriptures & Prayers for Deliverance from Trouble:

40 Days of Prayer for When Life Feels Overwhelming

Are you walking through a season where life feels heavy and your prayers feel weak?

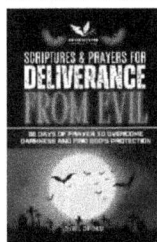

Scriptures & Prayers for Deliverance from Evil:

50 Days of Prayer to Overcome Darkness and Find God's Protection

When darkness presses in, how do you pray?

Scriptures & Prayers for Engaging the Enemy:

70 Days of Prayer to Rebuke the Enemy and Release God's Power

You weren't called to run from the battle—you were anointed to win it.

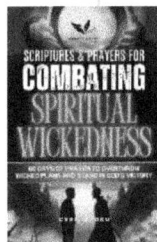

Scriptures & Prayers for Combating Spiritual Wickedness:

50 Days of Prayer to Overthrow Wicked Plans and Stand in God's Victory

Are you facing opposition that feels deeper than the natural? You're not imagining it—and you're not powerless.

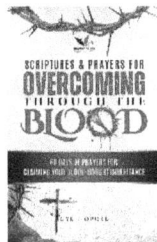

Scriptures & Prayers for Overcoming Through the Blood:

60 Days of Prayers for Claiming Your Blood-Bought Inheritance

You were never meant to fight sin, fear, or Satan in your own strength.

Standing in the Gap for Covenant Awakening:

30 Days of Prayer for National Repentance, Righteous Leadership & God's Sovereign Rule

What if your prayers could help turn the tide of a nation?

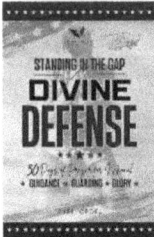

Standing in the Gap for Divine Defense:

30 Days of Prayer for National Guidance, Guarding & Glory

When the foundations of a nation feel as if they're shaking, prayer is the strongest fortress you can build.

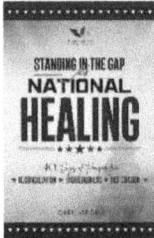

Standing in the Gap for National Healing:

40 Days of Prayer for Reconciliation, Righteousness, and Restoration

What if your prayers could help heal a nation? What if God is waiting for someone—like you—to stand in the gap?

Standing in the Gap for The President:

50 Days of Prayer for Leadership, Loyalty, and Lifeline

When a nation's leader is under spiritual siege, will you answer the call to stand in the gap?

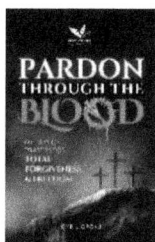

Pardon Through the Blood:

60 Days of Prayers for Total Forgiveness and Freedom

Guilt is a prison. The blood of Jesus holds the key.

Protection Through the Blood:

60 Days of Prayers for Living Untouchable Under Christ's Blood

You are not helpless. You are not exposed. You are covered—completely—by the blood of Jesus.

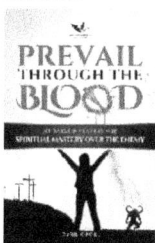

Prevail Through the Blood:

60 Days of Prayers for Spiritual Mastery Over the Enemy

What if every scheme of the enemy against your life could be dismantled—by one unstoppable weapon?

Preservation Through the Blood:

60 Days of Prayers for Divine Healing and Wholeness

Unlock Lasting Healing and Wholeness Through the Blood of Jesus

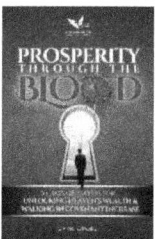

Prosperity Through the Blood:

60 Days of Prayers for Unlocking Heaven's Wealth and Walking in Covenant Increase

You were redeemed for more than survival—you were redeemed to prosper.

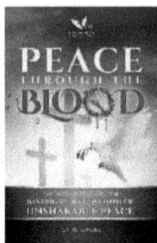

Peace Through the Blood:

60 Days of Prayers for Resting in the Covenant of Unshakable Peace

Are you ready to silence every storm of the mind, heart, and home—once and for all?

www.ingramcontent.com/pod-product-compliance
Lightning Source LLC
Chambersburg PA
CBHW062022040426
42447CB00010B/2105